M000207195

www.finishinglinepress.com

Crane Dance

poems by

Lois Levinson

Finishing Line Press
Georgetown, Kentucky

Crane Dance

ACKNOWLEDGMENTS

I thank the editors of these journals for publishing the following poems:

Bird's Thumb: "Ephemeral Pond"
Clementine Poetry Journal: "Flocked"
Mount Hope: "Murmuration", "Bird at Work" and "West of Ramona"
Yew: "On a Ragged Point"

My gratitude to John Brehm, whose teaching, critique and encouragement have
made this chapbook possible.

Publisher: Leah Maines

Editor: Christen Kincaid

Cover Art: Daniel Levinson

Author Photo: Mark Levinson

Cover Design: Daniel Levinson

Printed in the USA on acid-free paper.
Order online: www.finishinglinepress.com
          also available on amazon.com

Author inquiries and mail orders:
Finishing Line Press
P. O. Box 1626
Georgetown, Kentucky 40324
U. S. A.

Table of Contents

for Mark and Daniel

First Warbler of Spring

Along the creek
a miniscule star alights
in the cottonwoods,
and a sweet sweet
flute of song
takes wing.
I raise my binoculars.
There, on a low branch,
filling the frame,
a yellow warbler
tiny and roundish
and, oh so yellow—
dandelion yellow,
Crayola yellow,
as though all of
the world's yellow
had concentrated
in this one
small being.

Ephemeral Pond

A poem is taking shape in my brain
like an ephemeral pond after a storm,
an entire ecosystem that unfolds
in a place I thought was dry land.

Only yesterday I made my way through
withered grasses, suffered those desiccated
seeds with prickly edges that stick
to your shoes and poke through your socks.

Today in that very spot a pond emerges:
blue-winged teal and mallards dabble
in its waters, and snowy egrets
on black stilts step high at its shoreline.

Now a great blue heron glides in
to the water's edge, folds its impressive
wingspan and waits for the fish.
Can there be fish in an ephemeral pond?

Marsh grasses and reeds sprout up,
and frogs croak in the cattails.
Above the playa, dragonflies take flight,
and violet green swallows swoop and dive

for insects on the wing. Red-winged blackbirds
perch on reeds and croon their *po-poreeee.*
Unseen in the greenery, a tiny common
yellowthroat belts out his *witchety, witchety* aria.

I throw off my shoes and socks,
plunge my feet into the nascent water,
inhale its earthy scent, reach in to pluck
waterborne leaves and feel their slimy skins.

I must write the poem before it all vanishes.

West of Ramona

A row
of rural mailboxes
along the dirt road,
hodgepodge
of receptacles
tilted
at wacky angles,
unsteady
on their posts,
a gaggle
of crimsons,
jades,
cobalt blues,
mustard yellows,
crane their necks,
mouths agape
like nestlings
anxious
to be fed.

Waiting for the Roadrunner

He's a court jester of a bird,
wandering minstrel,
stand-up comic, traveller
from a sillier dimension,

a bird assembled from spare parts—
how else explain that wild crest
or the maniacal look in his eyes,
the absurd feet, the extravagant tail?

Consider his antics—cartoonlike,
he rushes in, stops short, peers
around corners, cocking his head,
then dashes off to his next gig.

Bird imitating art.

Some days you can catch him
sitting motionless in the sun,
his back feathers spread, absorbing
the sun's energy like a solar panel.

Recharged, he will vanish
into the brush, disappearing
so completely, you will doubt
you ever saw him.

They tell me the roadrunner
visits this cactus garden every afternoon.
I wait, feeling foolish to be keeping
an appointment with such a bird.

The roadrunner does not come.

Harlequin

Up and down the rocky coast
I searched for you
in tumultuous waves
that pummel the cliffs.

In the silvery mist
I scanned the surf
again and again
and waited.

Flotillas of dark birds swam by—
surf scoters with
outsized orange bills,
pigeon guillemots
kicking vermillion feet.

But you were not among them,
commedia dell'arte trickster,
harlequin duck,
Histrionicus histrionicus.

You left me hanging
over the edge of a cliff,
desperate for a glimpse
of a duck.

Bird at Work

A downy
woodpecker,
six inches
of determination,
red nape lit
like a taillight,
hangs upside
down from
a maple branch,
jackhammering
dead wood,
mining a vein
of insects,
his attention so
fixed on his work
he is unaware of me
beneath him,
looking up,
enthralled.

Crow Quandary

Some would call it a murder.
I prefer a Hitchcock of crows,

and it has gathered around my garbage can
this frigid morning, the overstuffed container

luring the birds to enjoy its marinated delights.
Still more crows arrive: they inspect, confer in clicks and rattles,

perch on the lid in twos and threes,
but the angled lid is icy, and there's little purchase.

They try to wedge the thing open,
but slide off, flap to the ground cawing.

Still others hop up and try; the group on the ground
urges them on with raucous cries.

I realize they're working together to solve the problem,
and that I want them to succeed.

In fact, I'm so invested in their process I forget about
the prospect of garbage strewn over the yard.

I remember the movie. Who knows what a Hitchcock might do?
I want to suggest—

Why don't two or three of you grab onto the lip of the lid
with your feet and then, together, flap your wings?

But, before they can seize on the solution, the garbage truck arrives,
all menace and roar, and the crows decamp,

the secrets of my household garbage secure for another week.

Flocked

I am being watched
by a flock of birds.
From above
I hear the high
tinkling bell sound
of bushtits, tiny grey
birds who zoom in
inches from my face,
then stuff themselves
into the suet feeder
by the dozens,
oblivious to my
outsized presence.
I can feel the small
wind of their wings.
Red-breasted nuthatches
swoop down, one, then
two, tooting like toy
trumpets, then an array
of chickadees chattering
to each other as they
snag their food—*over
here! It's better on
this side!*—they snatch
seeds and bounce off
to cache them in
the ponderosas.
A downy woodpecker
joins the foragers,
his red nape aflame
in the sunlight, close
enough for me to touch.
For a few perfect minutes
I am in this frenzied flock
of feeding birds.
I could be one of them,
as if this were an edge,

a threshold into a
dimension devoted
to the comings and
goings of birds,
invisible to most,
only *I* am granted
this brief passage
into their sphere.

Small Deaths

On a summer morning
laced with the scent
of sage I walk the grassy
meadows and scrub oak
of the ranchland,
making my weekly
check of bluebird nests.

I find four baby birds
dead in their nest,
bodies fused together.
Only one more week
and they would have
fledged, flown
free of the nest,
grown feathers
of an azure so intense
it could have been
torn from the sky.

If I were a scientist
I would record their loss,
submit my data,
and be done.
But these small deaths
fly out of my field notes,
slip past my armor,
and set loose specters

of those other lives
that might have been.

On a Ragged Point

I stand alone
on a ragged point
high above
a rocky shore.
Fogged in,
tucked in,
bony fingers
of cypress
cling to the edge.
Droplets make
the air palpable,
spider webs purled
by tendrils of mist,
dancing veils
of light and fog,
no hard edges,
no visible decay,
liquid silver
flowing.
Far below
the onslaught
of the tides,
relentless
bass of water
assaulting rock.
Otherworldly shapes
of cliffs emerge.
Tied neither
to earth
nor sea,
naked rock
floats free.
Above it all
the spiral aria
of the canyon wren.

Crane Fugue

Midwinter
in Bosque del Apache,
skeletal trees,
grasses faded
to honeyed brown,
thin crusts of ice
lace the ponds.
In this place
at the end of the day,
the sky gives up
its burden of cranes,
entrusting them
to the water
for the night.

Just at sunset
you can hear them
calling in their
ancient melodies,
myriad necklaces
of birds flying in
to roost,
sky poetry
approaching.
Then the lines
begin to bow,
breaking up into
individual
parachutes
which
descend
onto the
shoreline.

Sandhill cranes,
thousands of them,
balanced on stilts,

fold their wings,
extend extravagant
necks, reaching back
with ebony beaks
to arrange
the silvery bustles
of their tail feathers;
calling to each other
in clarinet trills,
they gather
their young
and wade into
shallow water
to sleep,
tucking their heads
into the soft pillows
of their backs.

At nightfall
two coyotes pace
the shore,
their prey
just out of reach.

Family Shooting

It's right there in the state park—
the sign along the road heralds
the Family Shooting Center,
which sounds, to me at least,
like a place you could bring the whole family—
ma, pa, granny, gramps, Billy and Susie,
and shoot them all.

It's hard to get used to the rattle
of gunfire as you walk the park trails,
looking and listening for birds.
You glimpse a tiny yellow warbler,
hear its delicate song, and
BOOM! the deep bass of gunfire
reverberates, and your brain
screams *Hit the ground!*

You know better, of course—
it's just those families
shooting one another—
but still… you've got to wonder
what the birds must be thinking.

Uncommon Ground

A golden eagle soars on a thermal,
and we stop to track its flight.

Women of a certain age,
our necks bent under the weight

of binoculars and cameras,
we sport floppy sun hats

and sensible shoes, our pockets lumpy
with water bottles and field guides.

We listen for bird sounds but hear instead
the rhythmic thud of boots on the trail.

Seven men move single file,
uniformed in camouflage,

solemn as soldiers
before battle, hunting rifles slung

over shoulders, faces smeared
with black war paint.

A darker, more sinister forest
passes through this one.

Snowy Egret

Swathed
in veils of
white plumes,
she steps
high through
shallows
on ebony
stilts,
heedless
of her
reflection.
Immersed
in fishing,
she focuses
hard on the
bottom,
her feet
probing
the mud
for prey.
Her wiggling
golden toes
must look
like fish
to the fish,
who never
see the
swift strike
of her
rapier
beak.

Murmuration

From a distance
you might mistake it
for a cloud of smoke
as it spreads across
the canvas
of prairie sky,
shape-shifting,
roiling, tumultuous,
first a dancing
funnel cloud,
then an elephant
rolling over,
a dragon rearing up,
a galaxy spinning,
then collapsing,
a phantasmagoria
formed by a myriad
of starlings locked
in labyrinthine ballet,
each image lasting
only an instant,
then dissolving,
as if a passage
to another universe
had revealed itself
and then vanished.

Hailstorm

On a September
afternoon the sky
churns up a storm cloud
the color of charcoal,
which descends
in a dousing of rain,
then a fusillade
of hailstones.
What was up
has come down—
tree branches,
shredded leaves,
roof shingles,
nails, crabapples,
frisbees,
tennis balls
strewn over
the yard.
Naked trees,
bludgeoned roofs,
battered cars,
shattered windows,
as if we needed
another lesson
in impermanence.
The house finch,
his song cut short,
washed away
from his roof perch
into the rain gutter,
down the downspout,
drowned.

Looking Up

Windy spring afternoon,
lake empty of birds,
iridescent flashes
of light high above,
like a miniature galaxy
visible in daytime,
so high I can barely
make sense of the shape.
I squint into the brightness,
try to organize this image
in my brain. Yes,
I know this pattern.
A troupe of white pelicans
dances on thermals,
wheels and spirals,
soars in flocks
that merge and split,
and merge and split again,
like a cell dividing,
as sunlight reflects
off their luminescent wings.
Disdaining the grey,
choppy waters of the lake,
they've flown aloft
to swim in air, frolic
on wind currents,
while I cling to the earth
in wonder.

Leafbirds

Leaves tumble
from already bare
maple branches.
As they touch the
ground, they
become birds—
red, and do I see
yellow ones?
Finches?
But packed
so tightly together
on a snowbank,
foraging with
such intensity that
I grab binoculars
to be sure.

Not house finches,
but red crossbills!
A nomadic flock
seeking pinecone seeds,
the males dull red,
the females yellow,
mountain birds
so rare in town,
landing for
a drink of snow
and a snack
outside my
front window,
materializing
like a poem.

Dancing with Cranes

In spring in Monte Vista
the sandhill cranes dance.
One bird begins, and the urge
to dance sweeps through the flock,
as though the earth
were rippling under their feet.

The long-legged birds bow
and leap, wings flapping
as if to shake off
the weight of winter,
then launch into jetés,
glides, pirouettes.

Mated pairs dance together,
hopeful males swagger
before the single ladies,
tentative youngsters watch,
then one by one, toe out
to make their own dance.

From the road, a gaggle of birders
observes through binoculars
and spotting scopes;
photographers with
artillery-sized lenses
capture the spectacle in pixels.

Only the poet sees that a passage
has opened to another world.
She climbs through the portal
onto the sandbar
into the flock
and joins the dance.

Three Moons

Moonrise silvers
the snowy Sangre de Cristos
as the last streaks of sunlight
turn fiery gold
the rough-hewn crosses
in the little graveyard
behind the pueblo church.

~

Blood Moon in eclipse,
so eerily crimson,
swollen, alien,
it could be
some celestial object
newly captured
by our planet's gravity,
not shining on its own,
but imbibing
its terracotta hue
from the Earth.

~

The full moon crouches
on the horizon,
yellow and inflated
as a second sun, then
pulls itself up
over the marsh
as seven sandhill cranes
cross in silhouette.

Owl Duet

For Mark

Call and response fly back and forth
on silent wings.

Will you come?
Yes, I will.

A great horned owl hoots
high in the blue spruce outside our window.

His deep bass resonates
against the mantle of darkness and snowfall.

Quiet, then an answering *hoo hoo*
from a distance.

Two owls duetting.
I imagine them an old mated pair

like us, only reunited mid-winter,
rekindling their bond,

while we, well past the anxieties
of nesting and raising young,

spend the evening
in our own call and response,

me writing this poem
for you.

Lois Levinson is a graduate of the Poetry Book Project at Lighthouse Writers Workshop in Denver, Colorado. Her poems have appeared in *Bird's Thumb, Clementine Poetry Journal, The Corner Club Press, These Fragile Lilacs, Mountain Gazette, The Literary Nest, Gravel, Literary Mama, Yew Journal* and *Mount Hope*. This is her first book.

CPSIA information can be obtained
at www.ICGtesting.com
Printed in the USA
LVOW12s0344261017
553827LV00001B/17/P